Pacific Economic Paper No. 198
August 1991

AGRICULTURAL DEVELOPMENT AND TRADE OF PACIFIC RIM COUNTRIES: TOWARDS THE 21ST CENTURY

Kym Anderson
Department of Economics &
Centre for International Economic Studies
University of Adelaide

Australia – Japan Research Centre

This paper is published under the direction of the Research Committee of the Australia–Japan Research Centre. The opinions expressed are those of the author and do not necessarily reflect the views of the Australia–Japan Research Centre.

The Australia–Japan Research Centre is part of the Research School of Pacific Studies in the Faculty of Economics at the Australian National University, Canberra, Australia.

ISSN 0728 8409
ISBN 0 86413 117 8

ABSTRACT

This paper examines the effects of economic growth in the Asia–Pacific region and elsewhere on agricultural production and trade of Pacific Rim countries. It reviews standard trade and development theory and shows that the past experience of Pacific Rim countries strongly supports that theory, particularly when account is taken of the distortions to incentives which government policies have imposed. Reasons are then canvassed for the pattern of distortions observed, which is that poor countries typically tax agriculture relative to other sectors but that as their economies develop, the policy regime gradually changes from taxing to increasingly assisting farmers. With this understanding of the determinants of both comparative advantage and distortions to incentives over time, and some assertions about prospective rates of economic growth of Pacific Rim countries, an assessment is made as to the likely future pattern of Pacific trade in farm products. The paper concludes with a discussion of how this pattern might be affected by a series of policy developments. These include the Uruguay Round negotiations, the trend towards regionalism in Europe and elsewhere, and the greening of world politics.

CONTENTS

LIST OF TABLES

Introduction

The question of what impact economic growth in Pacific Rim countries and elsewhere will have on the agricultural trade of those economies is naturally of great importance to agricultural exporters in countries such as Australia, Canada, New Zealand, Thailand and the United States. It is also of great interest, however, to people in densely populated, newly industrialising nations who fear that their agricultural sector and food security will decline as farmers become less competitive in the wake of industrialisation. An all-too-common response to that fear is a call for protection from food import competition. When the call is heeded the protection inevitably is deemed insufficient, and so the escalation of agricultural protection begins. This in turn raises domestic food prices and reduces trade growth, thereby frustrating both domestic consumers and non-food exporters, not to mention overseas producers of farm products.

Thus, to understand likely developments in agricultural production and trade it is necessary to look at the determinants of not only agricultural comparative advantage but also policy distortions to incentives facing producers and consumers in each economy as it grows.

The first section of this paper briefly reviews standard trade and development theory as it applies to the agricultural sector of a growing economy. It shows that while it is virtually inevitable that agriculture's share of production and employment will decline with economic growth, the same is not necessarily true of agriculture's share of exports or of food self-sufficiency — even in an economy which remains undistorted. The latter is therefore even less likely in an economy whose growth is accompanied by policy changes which favour increasingly the farm sector, as Western Europe clearly demonstrates. The second section examines the extent to which empirical evidence from Pacific Rim countries supports the standard theory. It turns out their experiences conform very closely with that theory, particularly when account is taken of the changes to distortionary policies affecting farmers' incentives.

We often observe policies which discriminate against agriculture in poor countries and favour farmers in rich countries. Reasons for this gradual change, which tends to increasingly favour agriculture as an economy develops, are briefly canvassed in the third section. This understanding of the political economy of policy trends, together with the empirically supported theory of changing comparative advantages, makes it possible to say something in the final section about future prospects, both for traditional agricultural-exporting countries as well as for newly industrialising countries and those contemplating major policy reforms.

Conceptualising agricultural development in a growing economy

Why agriculture's relative importance declines

Why does the agricultural sector tend to decline in relative importance over time? When domestic savings accumulate or foreign capital flows in from abroad in the form of grants or loans, the economy's production possibilities expand and incomes rise. More is thus spent on the available goods, but not in the same proportions as before. In particular, the demand for essentials such as food rises relatively slowly (Engel's Law). In a closed economy — including the world as a whole — this Engel effect means that economic growth will be accompanied by a decline in the price of food relative to non-food products, *ceteris paribus*.[1] Any small open economy faced with such a price decline in world markets will tend to move resources out of agriculture into sectors producing other tradables. Also, as incomes grow in this economy the demand for non-tradables tends to grow more than proportionately and thereby cause resources to be attracted to their production.[2] Thus both the relative price and the relative quantity of farm products tend to decline as incomes grow at home and abroad, and so too, therefore, does agriculture's shares of GDP and employment.

The only situation in which this would not happen in a small open economy is if output growth is sufficiently biased in favour of agriculture to offset the relative price decline for farm products. That requires either total factor productivity growth to be faster in agriculture than in other sectors, and/or the endowment of factors used relatively intensively in farming (most notably agricultural land) to increase relatively rapidly.[3] This is likely to be especially difficult to achieve in densely populated economies.

Must agricultural self-sufficiency also decline?

What determines whether a country is a net agricultural exporter or importer at a point in time? And how will that position change with economic growth at home and abroad? A modification by Krueger (1977)[4] of the standard theory of comparative advantage suggests that when a poor economy opens up to international trade, its exports initially will be specialised in primary products, because its stocks on non-farm capital relative to farm capital (principally land) are comparatively low. The proportion of those primary exports that is agricultural will be larger, the greater this country's endowment of agricultural land relative to minerals compared with that ratio globally. If the country's domestic incomes and non-farm capital to labour ratio grow more rapidly than the rest of the world's (for example, because of a high domestic savings ratio or large borrowings from abroad),[5] its export specialisation will gradually switch away from primary products (in raw or lightly processed form) to manufactures, in the absence of distortionary policies. This switch will begin at an earlier stage of economic development, and the manufactured goods initially exported will be more labour-intensive, the more resource-poor or densely populated the country (population density serving as a crude inverse proxy for the stock of agricultural land and minerals per worker). Since many textile and clothing production activities tend to be intensive in the use of unskilled labour, this theory suggests they will be among the items initially exported by a newly industrialising, densely populated country, and that as the demand for textile raw materials by that country's expanding textile industry grows, so the country's net exports of natural fibre will diminish, or net imports of natural fibre will increase, *ceteris paribus*.

These smooth changes in comparative advantage can of course be disrupted by sudden shocks to the economy, such as a major institutional or relative price change. The introduction in rural China of large communes in 1958 and of the household responsibility system and huge producer price hikes in the late 1970s are cases in point. Other examples are a sustained change in the international terms of trade for a country, such as happened with the petroleum price increases of 1973 and 1979–80 and their decrease in the mid-1980s before jumping again in late 1990, and a discovery of new mineral deposits (Corden 1984).

Empirical support for the theory

Global cross-sectional evidence

This theory has strong empirical support from both cross-sectional and time-series evidence.[6] The negative relationship between agriculture's shares of GDP, employment (EMP) and exports (EXP) on the one hand, and income per capita (YPC) on the other, are very significant statistically. These shares are also negatively associated with population density per unit of agricultural land (PDA), although significantly so only for the export share equation. This is

Table 1 Population, national product and trade orientation of Pacific Rim economies

	Population, 1987		GNP, 1987 (US$ billion)	GNP per capita		Ratio of exports to GDP (%)		Share (%) of world agricultural trade, 1987	
	Total (millions)	Per unit of agricultural land[a]		US$ 1987	Real growth rate (% p.a.) 1965–86	1960	1986	Exports	Imports
	(1)	(2)	(3)	(4)	(5)	(6)	(7)	(8)	(9)
Northeast Asian market economies									
Japan	122	21.8	1,926	15,770	4.3	11	12	0.7	11.2
Hong Kong	6	>100	45	8,260	6.2	82	112	0.1	1.7
South Korea	43	17.9	113	2,690	6.7	3	41	0.8	1.8
Taiwan	20	20.0	108	5,400	6.9	11	61	1.1	1.5
Southeast Asian market economies									
Indonesia	172	5.0	77	500	4.6	13	21	0.4	1.7
Malaysia	16	3.4	29	1,800	4.3	54	57	0.5	1.9
Philippines	58	5.9	34	590	1.9	11	25	0.2	0.5
Singapore	3	>100	20	7,940	7.6	163	na	0.9	0.9
Thailand	53	2.4	45	840	4.0	17	27	1.7	0.4
East Asian centrally planned economies									
China	1,086	2.8	600[b]	580[b]	5.1	4	11	2.4	1.3
Kampuchea	8	0.7	na	na	na	na	na	0.0	0.0
North Korea	21	8.3	na	na	na	na	na	0.1	0.0
Laos	4	2.1	na	na	na	na	na	0.0	0.0
Vietnam	63	8.7	na	na	na	na	na	0.1	0.1
Australasia									
Australia	16	0.03	176	10,900	1.7	15	16	3.1	0.6
New Zealand	3	0.2	27	8,230	1.5	22	29	1.6	0.2
North America									
Canada	26	0.3	390	15,080	2.6	18	27	6.0	2.1
United States	246	0.4	4,486	18,430	1.6	5	7	12.6	10.9
Mexico	83	0.8	149	1,820	2.6	10	16	0.8	0.6

Notes: na not available.

a Agricultural land area per capita (arable land plus permanent crops and pastures) in the country shown relative to that in the rest of the world.

b Based on Perkins' (1988) estimate that China's per capita income in 1985 was US$500.

Sources: World Bank (1988a, 1988b); FAO, *Production Yearbook*, and *Trade Yearbook*, Rome, 1988; Council on Economic Planning and Development, *Taiwan Statistical Data Book*, Taipei, 1988; International Economic Data Bank, *World Trade Tapes*, ANU, Canberra, 1990.

clear from the following OLS regression equations, from Anderson (1987), which are based on World Bank data for 1981 for 70 countries with populations in excess of one million (t-values in parentheses):

$$(1) \quad GDP = 87 - 9.2 \ln YPC \underset{(6.7)}{} \qquad \bar{R}^2 = 0.80$$

$$(2) \quad EMP = 179 - 18.5 \ln YPC \underset{(6.6)}{} \qquad \bar{R}^2 = 0.82$$

$$(3) \quad EXP = 152 - 9.5 \ln YPC - 8.5 \ln PDA \qquad \bar{R}^2 = 0.45$$

(t-values: (5.1) for lnYPC, (4.7) for lnPDA)

As well, the theory suggests that the share of labour-intensive manufactures such as textile and clothing in total manufactured exports (TEX) would be very high at first as income per capita (YPC) increases from a low base and then would fall, and would tend to be higher the greater the population density of the country (PD) — a crude index of the endowment of natural resources per capita suggested by Keesing and Sherk (1977), Bowen (1983) and Leamer (1984). Evidence supporting this can be obtained by estimating an OLS regression equation from cross-sectional data. For example, using the data available for the year 1986 from the World Bank (1988a) for 63 countries with populations exceeding one million, the following equation is estimated:

$$TEX = 25.6 + 7.77 \ln YPC - .523 (\ln YPC)^2 + .163 PD, \qquad \bar{R}^2 = 0.52$$

(t-values: (5.6), (5.7), (6.3))

These equations are clearly consistent with the theory of development and changing comparative advantage summarised above.

Time-series evidence from Pacific Rim countries

Time-series evidence is also strongly supportive of the above theory of structural change and comparative advantage in growing economies. What is clear from columns 2 and 5 of Table 1 is that Northeast Asia's market economies and Singapore are extremely poorly endowed with agricultural land per worker and have enjoyed extremely rapid incomes growth during

Table 2 Declining importance of agriculture in Northeast Asia, 1880 to 1987

	Share of agriculture (%) in:		
	Employment	Domestic products	Exports
Japan			
1880	74	38	63
1900	60	29	30
1920	51	22	23
1939	42	15	18
1960	33	13	11
1970	19	6	5
1980	11	4	2
1987	8	3	1
South Korea			
1956	na	46	89
1960	66	40	56
1970	50	26	17
1980	34	15	10
1987	20	12	5
Taiwan			
1953	56	38	92
1960	50	33	68
1970	37	18	21
1980	20	9	9
1987	15	6	6
China [a]			
1946	na	68	na
1952	84	58	na
1957	81	47	55
1962	82	48	na
1967	82	48	na
1972	80	38	47
1978	71	33	34
1984	64	40	23
1987	60	34	18

Notes: na not available.
a Some of the Chinese data refer to the average of several years centred on the year shown.
Source: Anderson (1990, Tables 2.1, 3.4, 3.6 & 3.7).

Table 3 Indexes of 'revealed' comparative advantage[a] in agriculture and in textiles and clothing in East Asia, 1899 to 1987

	Agriculture	Textiles and clothing
Japan		
1899	>1.0	1.5
1913	0.7	2.6
1929	0.7	2.9
1937	0.5	4.1
1954–56	0.4	5.5
1964–66	0.3	2.7
1971–73	0.2	1.7
1976–78	0.2	1.0
1982–84	0.1	0.7
1985–87	0.1	0.5
Hong Kong		
1954–56	na	5.4
1964–66	na	7.0
1971–73	na	7.6
1976–78	na	9.2
1982–84	na	7.2
1985–87	na	6.7
South Korea		
1954–56	2.7	na
1964–66	1.6	4.3
1971–73	0.7	6.3
1976–78	0.6	6.6
1982–84	0.5	4.8
1985–87	0.4	3.9
Taiwan		
1954–56	2.6	na
1964–66	2.1	2.2
1971–73	0.8	4.8
1976–78	0.7	5.0
1982–84	0.6	4.1
1985–87	0.5	2.9
China		
1955–59	na	2.1
1965–69	2.1	3.3
1975–77	2.2	3.9
1978–80	1.9	4.6
1981–83	1.6	5.0
1984–87	1.4	5.1
ASEAN[b]		
1965–69	2.6	0.3
1970–74	2.5	0.5
1975–79	2.3	0.6
1980–84	1.9	0.7
1985–87	1.9	1.1

Notes: na not available.

a Share of an economy's exports due to these commodities relative to those commodities' share in total world exports, following Balassa (1965). Agriculture is defined as SITC sections 0, 10, 2 (excluding 27, 28) and 4; textiles and clothing include SITC division 65 and 84.

b Brunei, Indonesia, Malaysia, Philippines, Singapore and Thailand.

Source: Anderson (1990, Tables 2.3 & 3.8).

Table 4 Declining importance of agriculture in the United States and Australia, 1830 to 1989

	Share of agriculture (%) in:		
	Employment	Domestic products	Exports
United States			
1830	71	na	85 (22)
1850	55	na	83 (21)
1870	53	35	81 (25)
1890	43	24	79 (42)
1910	31	16	55 (20)
1930	22	11	36 (14)
1950	12	6	33 (14)
1970	4	4	22 (11)
1987	3	2	na
Australia			
1910	24	24	76
1930	24	21	87
1950	13	24	89
1960	10	13	78
1970	8	7	53
1980	6	7	45
1989	5	5	37
OECD average			
1960	22	7	23
1987	8	3	12

Notes: na not available.
a The US export data refer to all primary products, with food only shown in parentheses.
Sources: US Department of Commerce (1976); OECD (1989); Freebairn (1987); Keating (1973); ABARE (1990).

the past 25 years; the other economies of East Asia have grown moderately rapidly and are moderately densely populated (China more so than is indicated because three-quarters of its agricultural land is low-quality pastoral land); and that Australasia and North America are extremely well endowed with farm land per worker and their economic growth has been relatively sluggish.

This categorisation is not to suggest that there is a causative link between income growth and population density, although there may be indirectly, in the sense that economies extremely poorly endowed in natural resources have to trade more and their openness enhances economic growth (compare columns 2, 5 and 7 of Table 1). This categorisation aims to examine the extent to which the theory in the first section of the paper is supported by the changing production and trade pattern of these three groups of economies.[7]

Specifically, the theory leads one to expect that the relative importance of agriculture in Japan and its densely populated and rapidly growing neighbours will decline rapidly, and that these countries will lose comparative advantage in farm products but gain it in (initially labour-intensive) manufactures. One would also anticipate similar though less rapid changes for the other market economies of East Asia, and a slower decline in agricultural competitiveness for Australasia and North America, with a lingering comparative advantage in farm products despite their advanced income status (Mexico excepted).

This is indeed what has occurred. Table 2 shows the extremely rapid decline in the relative importance of agriculture in Northeast Asia — including China even before the reforms began in 1978 but especially since then. In Indonesia and Thailand, too, agriculture's share of GDP has halved during the past two decades. The international competitiveness of East Asian agriculture also has declined rapidly, as shown in Table 3. The importance of agriculture in these economies' exports was more than twice the world average at the time they began to industrialise, but its relative importance has fallen precipitously. In Japan and the four NIEs of Hong Kong, Singapore, South Korea and Taiwan, farm products now constitute only a small fraction of their exports relative to agriculture's share of world exports. And even for the other ASEAN countries and China that ratio (the 'revealed' comparative advantage index) is fast approaching unity. Conversely, manufacturing exports have become increasingly more important for these economies, beginning with labour-intensive products such as textiles and clothing before moving to more skill and technology-intensive products (see column 2 of Table 3).

For countries well endowed with agricultural land such as the United States and Australia, agriculture's share of exports is well above the OECD average and has declined much less rapidly than in East Asia, as expected. But, as Table 4 shows, agriculture's shares of employment and national product have nonetheless declined quite rapidly, and to the very low levels of other OECD countries. This supports the theory which suggests that retaining a degree of international competitiveness is insufficient to prevent a decline in the importance of agriculture in the domestic economy. That is, even the most advantaged agricultural sectors are not immune from the need for structural adjustment of resources out of farming. Those adjustments are accentuated in the face of a minerals export boom, such as Australia faced from the late 1960s to early 1980s (see especially column 3 of Table 4). Farmers in Canada,

Table 5 Importance, competitiveness and land productivity of agriculture in Pacific Rim economies, 1965 to 1988 (per cent)

	Share of agriculture in:						Index of 'revealed' comparative advantage in:				Grain yield per ha 1986–88[b]		
	Employment		Domestic Products		Exports		Agriculture		Textiles and clothing		Rice	Wheat	Coarse grain
	1965	1980	1965	1988	1965	1988	1965	1988	1965	1988			
Northeast Asia													
China	81	74	44	32	48	17	1.8	1.2	3.4	3.8	1.6	1.3	1.4
Japan	26	11	9	3	7	1	0.2	0.1	2.7	0.3	1.9	1.5	1.2
South Korea	55	34	38	11	25	5	0.9	0.4	4.3	3.2	1.9	1.4	1.1
Taiwan	47	20	27	6	54	6	2.1	0.4	2.3	2.4	1.1	1.5	
Southeast Asia													
Indonesia	71	57	56	24	53	22	2.0	1.5	0.0	1.2	1.2	–	0.8
Malaysia	59	42	28	21	59	37	2.2	2.6	0.0	0.8	–	–	
Philippines	58	52	26	23	84	26	3.1	1.9	0.1	1.1	0.8	–	0.5
Thailand	82	71	32	17	84	45	3.2	3.2	0.1	2.6	0.6	–	0.9
North America / Australasia													
Australia	10	7	9	4	73	38	2.7	2.7	0.1	0.1	2.1	0.6	0.6
Canada	10	5	6	4	35	20	1.3	1.4	0.1	0.1	–	0.8	1.3
Mexico	50	37	14	9	62	7	2.3	0.5	0.4	0.3	1.1	1.8	0.9
New Zealand	13	11	na	10	94	68	3.5	4.9	0.0	0.3	–	1.8	2.0
United States	5	4	3	2	27	17	1.0	1.2	0.4	0.3	1.9	1.0	2.3

Notes: na not available.

a Share of an economy's exports due to these commodities relative to those commodities' share in total world exports.

b Yield in the country shown as a ratio of the global average.

Sources: World Bank (1988a, 1990); International Economic Data Bank, *World Trade Tapes*, ANU, Canberra, 1990.

Indonesia, Malaysia and Mexico also were adversely affected by currency appreciation following the growth in their energy export earnings in the 1970s and early 1980s, and will be again if the petroleum price rise in late 1990 is sustained.

The extent of the adjustments made by other Pacific Rim economies since 1965 are summarised in Table 5, along with indexes of their international competitiveness in agriculture and textiles and their land productivity. Southeast Asia has adjusted away from agriculture less rapidly and from a higher base than Northeast Asia's market economies, as expected given its lower economic growth rates and population density, but the adjustment has nonetheless been substantial. The final three columns of Table 5 show that the loss in competitiveness is not necessarily correlated with crop yields per hectare. Indeed, Northeast Asia has relatively high yields, reflecting the fact that government incentives encourage the heavy use of yield-enhancing inputs such as fertiliser and pesticides.

As incomes rise in developing countries, the demand for livestock products and fruit and vegetables tends to rise by at least the same proportion, while the demand for staples rises much more slowly. Fruit and vegetable production and intensive livestock production (pork, chicken and eggs) require relatively little land per dollar of output. Fresh fruit and vegetables, in addition, often enjoy natural protection from foreign competition because of their perishable nature, as does fluid milk.[8] Thus countries facing a declining comparative advantage in agriculture in general may nonetheless be able to profitably switch some farm resources into these activities. While this would reduce the need to import these items, it is likely that a large-scale expansion in intensive livestock production would necessitate increased dependence on imported feedgrains. In Northeast Asia, for example, exactly these types of changes have occurred. The shares of livestock products and fruit and vegetables in the gross value of their agricultural production have increased substantially at the expense of cereals over the past 30 years (Table 6). And self-sufficiency of intensive livestock products has been maintained at close to 100 per cent while that of feedstuffs, especially corn and soybean, has fallen dramatically, as it has for wheat and for beef to a lesser extent (Table 7). Similar trends have also occurred in other countries. Mexico in particular has expanded its production of fruit and vegetables to satisfy not only domestic demand growth but also growing US import demand. In this case production is occurring close to the land border and the lower labour costs in Mexico provide it with a comparative advantage over the United States in producing these relatively labour-intensive foods. The bottom of Table 7 shows, however, that despite the decline in agriculture's relative importance in the economies of

Southeast Asia, ASEAN's food self-sufficiency has been maintained, thanks to rapid farm output growth in Indonesia and Thailand.

Table 6 Composition of farm household income in Japan, South Korea and Taiwan, 1955 to 1987 (per cent)

	Share of gross value of farm output[a] from:				Share of valued added in the gross value of farm output
	Grain	Livestock products	Fruit and vegetables	Other	
Japan					
1955–59	58	12	17	13	na
1960–64	50	18	20	12	68
1965–69	46	20	21	13	67
1970–74	37	25	26	12	63
1975–79	38	26	26	10	60
1980–84	31	28	26	15	53
1985–86	32	26	26	16	53
South Korea					
1955–59	na	na	na	na	na
1960–64	78	7	6	9	na
1965–69	60	13	13	14	na
1970–74	57	14	15	14	81
1975–79	53	16	22	11	78
1980–84	40	25	24	11	74
1985–87	42	25	26	7	67
Taiwan					
1955–59	56	20	7	17	66
1960–64	55	22	9	14	64
1965–69	46	26	13	15	63
1970–74	39	33	18	10	56
1975–79	34	36	20	10	54
1980–84	25	38	27	10	50
1985–87	21	40	28	11	49

Notes: na not available.
a Valued at current domestic prices.
Source: Anderson (1990, Table 4.11).

Table 7 Agricultural self-sufficiency and agricultural protection in Northeast Asia, 1961 to 1986

	Self-sufficiency index (production as a percentage of apparent consumption):									Average nominal rate of protection[b]
	Wheat	Coarse grain	Soybean	Rice	Beef & sheepmeat	Pork & poultry	Dairy products	Sugar	Weighted average[a]	
Japan										
1961–64	30	36	20	97	66	99	92	24	78	68
1965–69	20	19	8	109	51	97	90	27	77	87
1970–74	6	5	4	94	51	95	90	20	67	110
1975–79	5	3	4	110	45	92	87	20	67	147
1980–84	11	2	4	92	51	91	86	31	64	151
1985–86	14	2	–	107	52	90	88	34	67	na
South Korea										
1961–64	20	87	89	100	100	100	26	0	92	3
1965–69	18	98	94	94	99	100	54	0	86	18
1970–74	7	68	81	91	89	102	85	0	77	75
1975–79	3	40	66	96	69	100	97	0	75	146
1980–84	3	22	58	93	69	100	96	0	69	195
1985–86	0	13	50	98	96	100	99	0	69	239
Taiwan										
1961–64	9	25	29	103	100	100	38	253	120	2
1965–69	5	16	20	105	100	100	33	254	115	2
1970–74	0	6	9	100	70	103	28	252	97	17
1975–79	0	4	5	111	16	103	23	187	85	36
1980–84	0	4	4	119	5	103	22	147	77	57
1985–86	0	7	1	104	5	107	29	125	77	na
China										
1961–64	80	97	103	104	100	101	100	48	98	na
1965–69	86	101	104	103	101	102	100	78	100	na
1970–74	93	104	101	105	101	102	100	79	102	na
1975–79	96	103	99	104	101	101	99	72	101	na
1980–84	86	100	101	101	103	101	99	76	98	na
1985–86	87	96	108	100	104	101	98	80	96	na
ASEAN										
1961–64	0	118	94	102	96	100	13	171	104	na
1965–69	0	133	91	105	95	100	12	151	105	na
1970–74	0	133	89	101	92	100	14	164	104	na
1975–79	0	127	70	1403	90	101	14	169	105	na
1980–84	0	126	47	109	93	102	18	153	109	na
1985–86	0	132	57	110	88	103	28	143	109	na

Notes: na not available.
a Weights based on value of domestic production at border prices.
b The percentage by which the domestic producer price for grain and meat exceeds the international price at the country's border. The final period shown for Japan and Taiwan is 1980–82 and that for Korea is 1985.

Source: Anderson (1990, Table 2.4).

The role of policy interventions

Trends in the inter-sectoral pattern of production and trade depend not only on changes in comparative advantage but also on trends in the distortions to incentives due to government policies. There is ample evidence to suggest that advanced industrial economies tend to subsidise agriculture relative to other sectors, while developing countries tend to effectively tax farm relative to non-farm producers (Schultz 1978; Anderson 1989). This suggests that the incentive structure which is distorted against agriculture in low-income countries may gradually be altered by governments to increasingly favour farmers as economic growth occurs. This has happened steadily in Western Europe, and has occurred even faster in Japan and extremely rapidly in Korea and Taiwan (Anderson, Hayami and others 1986).

There are good politico-economic reasons for expecting such a trend in policy. They have to do with the income distributional effects of distortionary policies in rich as compared with poor countries, as well as changes in the costs of collective action by different groups and in the preferences of society. On preferences, it is not difficult to understand why a poor agrarian society may wish to encourage the infant industrial sector to 'modernise', while in a rich industrial society people would be sympathetic to the small farm sector as it struggles to survive. The public may even judge that farm subsidies are a necessary price to pay to ensure political stability. But the distributional effects of policy choices and the relative costs of collective action by lobby groups in the two different types of economies are no doubt the main driving forces behind the observed pattern of distortions, for the following reasons.

If one were to assume that capital (including land) is sector specific and labour is the only mobile resource, then the distributional effects of altering the relative price of farm products depends importantly on its impacts on wage costs and on the share of the community's expenditure on food. In a poor economy where most people work in agriculture, raising the relative price of agricultural products has a large impact on the demand for labour, thereby raising wage rates substantially. This erodes much of the gain to landholders, and yet will be insufficient to offset the increase in the cost of living for labourers. Even more importantly, it reduces very substantially the income of industrial capitalists. These effects, plus the fact that farmers have much greater free-rider and other costs of getting together to lobby collectively than do urban groups, ensure there is a relatively weak demand for agricultural assistance policies relative to demands for industrial-sector assistance in poor agrarian economies.

In rich industrial economies, on the other hand, agriculture is a small employer and so raising the relative price of farm products has little impact on the demand for labour and hence wages. And since people spend much less of their income on farm products in these as compared with poor economies, the product price change affects the cost of living by less. Hence other groups, including industrial capitalists, have little incentive to oppose agricultural support policies in advanced economies.

When typical values for these and other parameters are included in a computable general equilibrium model of a poor agrarian economy and a rich industrial one, the income distributional effects of policy intervention contrast markedly. A simulation exercise by Anderson (1989) suggests that a 10 per cent increase in the price of farm products would raise farmers' real incomes by only 4 per cent in the 'typical' poor country but would reduce the real incomes of industrial capitalists by 43 per cent, while the same policy shock in the 'typical' rich country raises farmers' real incomes by 23 per cent while lowering those of industrial capitalists by only 3 per cent. And the real incomes of non-farm workers would be lowered by four times as much (2.5 per cent) in the poor country as in the rich one; hence they too would be more inclined to join industrialists in opposing an increase in the relative price of food in the poor country, possibly by rioting.

While this is far from the full story, it goes some way towards explaining why one observes farm subsidies in rich countries but disincentives for agriculture in poor countries. It suggests that the tendency observed in Western Europe and Northeast Asia for policies to gradually change from discouraging agriculture to excessively encouraging it in the course of economic development may occur in subsequent generations of NIEs too. Moreover, there tends to be a strong negative correlation also between agricultural protection and agricultural comparative advantage.[9] This suggests densely populated countries are likely to switch from being more to being less than fully self-sufficient in farm products at a slower rate than one might expect from the theory of comparative advantage alone. As discussed in the final section of this paper, however, international political pressures may moderate slightly the domestic political pressures generating these policy trends (Lee, Hadwinger & Lee 1990).

Future economic growth and policy reform prospects

Overall, the agricultural production and trade trends in Pacific Rim countries strongly support standard trade and development theory. Certainly, there are many price and trade policies in place which distort trade in farm products, but in this region they tend to have merely weakened the degree of specialisation and slowed the rate of decline of agriculture and the associated change in trade patterns. This allows one to use that theory with some confidence in speculating about likely future developments. In general, if relative economic growth rates continue as in the recent past, many of the trends in agricultural production and trade noted above will continue into the next century, around which there will no doubt be fluctuations due to weather and short-term policy changes. But to be more precise requires first assessing the longer-run growth prospects of economies within (and beyond) the region.[10]

Prospective economic growth rates

Future economic growth rates will depend in large part on the attitudes and policy choices made in the various countries of the world. Japan and the East Asian NIEs have several characteristics which are conducive to continued rapid output and hence income growth. One is the high value placed on formal education and on-the-job training, which ensures the workforce is not only relatively highly skilled but also adaptable. Another is the capacity for social cohesion, which is manifest in the widespread acceptance of the ideology of economic growth and the preparedness of people to accept the inconvenient disruptions to life that necessarily accompany rapid growth. Third, their postwar land reforms ensured an unusually equitable distribution of that important source of wealth. That fact, together with the necessary dependence on the productive use of labour in export-oriented manufacturing for output growth (in the absence of an abundance of natural resources), has ensured a remarkably equitable growth in incomes in these densely populated economies as real wages have risen. This growth has been facilitated not only by the exceptionally high propensity to save and invest but also by a willingness to import ideas, technology and other forms of capital from abroad, a preparedness to let market forces generally dictate the allocation of productive resources, and a political environment which supports investors with long-term horizons. It is true that the politics of these countries may be somewhat less stable in the 1990s than in recent decades, particularly as their labour markets tighten and their large current account surpluses decrease, but these changes are likely to have only a minor rather than a major dampening effect on their economic growth rates (Garnaut 1989).

China has several of these characteristics and during the decade from late 1978 it had most of them. Not surprisingly, that decade was one of very rapid economic growth. The growth rate was exceptionally high, partly because the take-off was from a low starting point in terms of real wages and levels of technology, marketing and other management skills. Thus by liberalising its domestic markets, opening up to trade and allowing new ideas, technical know-how, financial capital and the like to be imported, the payoff was enormous. It would continue to be so for years to come should the government return to the economic reform agenda that in the late 1980s was put aside, especially in urban areas where reforms still have a long way to go. Moreover, a return to the agenda of gradually adopting market forces in China also would have positive spin-offs to growth in Hong Kong and to a lesser extent Taiwan, where investors are understandably nervous about the uncertainty in China's attitudes towards those territories as 1997 approaches.

For the rapid growth of these East Asian economies to continue in the long term, a continuing program of policy liberalisation is required, according to Krueger (1990). It also helps to have favourable terms of trade. The low prices of primary products in international markets during most of the 1980s, particularly for energy, benefited resource-poor economies substantially.[11] At the same time, surplus savings have benefited from high interest rates abroad. Low primary product prices may well continue in the absence of major policy changes, discussed below, but earnings from the export of financial capital are less certain. On the one hand, the ageing of Japan's population and the lower savings rates of its young workers are likely to reduce the supply of Japanese funds in international markets, at a time when the reconstruction of East European economies will increase the demand for such funds. On the other hand, as Klein (1990) points out, the ending of the Cold War — which is making Eastern Europe's reform and reconstruction programs possible — will reduce the world's demand for funds for military investments. Only time will tell what the net effect of these forces — and of the Gulf crisis of late 1990, should it be prolonged — will be on world interest rates and thereby on the growth rates of East Asian (and other) economies.

The end of the Cold War and the growth performance of China in the early 1980s may encourage Asia's other centrally planned economies to open up. Already Vietnam is moving in that direction, a political settlement of the Cambodian issue seems closer, and even North Korea might eventually open up following the recent historic meeting between Presidents Gorbachev and Noh. Given their enormous scope for profitably importing foreign technology and capital, the potential is there for these socialist economies too to double their output in a decade, just as China did when it opened up in 1978, or at least to achieve the moderately fast growth rates of the ASEAN economies.

North America and Australasia may grow a little faster in the 1990s than in the 1980s because of the formation of their respective free-trade areas, but substantial changes from the relatively low growth rates of the past would require major reforms to their economic policies. It is expected that New Zealand's experiment with such reforms in the latter 1980s will bear fruit from the early 1990s if its reform process is allowed to continue. Australia is following New Zealand's example only to a minor extent: rapid growth there will not occur without substantial reductions in manufacturing protection, privatisation of state enterprises and major reductions in the regulation of markets for labour and various services. In North America, too, growth is dampened to some extent by the continued use of trade interventions aimed to appease powerful vested interest groups in agriculture, manufacturing and services.

Likely trends in agricultural production and trade

Given these expectations about future economic growth rates, theory and past experience make it possible to anticipate the broad trends in future production and trade in farm products. Japan and the four NIEs of East Asia are likely to become ever-larger importers of wheat, corn and soybean as well as tropical agricultural products. However, wheat products will grow less rapidly than in the past as income and population growth rates slow down and per capita consumption levels approach saturation point. Furthermore, growth in corn and soybean imports will depend crucially on whether the high levels of protection currently afforded meat (especially beef) and dairy products are raised further or lowered in the years ahead. In the latter event, discussed in the next section, imports of livestock products would substitute for imports of feedstuffs, and per capita consumption of meat and milk could rise substantially given their current relatively low levels (Table 8). Rice imports are unlikely to rise, unless a substantial liberalisation of the rice market results from the Uruguay Round.

Japan's share of world imports of cotton and wool has been falling during the past decade, but it has been more than offset by the increase in the shares due to the Northeast Asian NIEs and, until the late 1980s, to China. As a region Northeast Asia now imports more than one third of the world's natural fibre trade. This trend can be expected to continue through the 1990s, although if China were to open up its markets more then an increasing share of those imports would be used for producing textile and clothing exports from China rather than from the NIEs (Anderson 1991).

The ASEAN economies are likely to continue to lose comparative advantage in agriculture, but from a high base. To date, their self-sufficiency in temperate food products

Table 8 Per capita consumption of grain and livestock products, Pacific Rim economies, 1961 to 1986 (kg per capita per year)

		Grains		Soybean products	Meat	Dairy products	Eggs
		Direct	Indirect[a]				
Japan	1961–64	181	38	48	8	29	11
	1985–86	156	117	93	36	69	18
N.E. Asian NIEs	1961–64	245	7	19	10	1	4
	1985–86	246	175	119	39	28	13
China	1961–64	139	11	20	5	3	2
	1985–86	243	44	21	19	5	6
ASEAN	1961–64	138	4	3	6	3	2
	1985–86	169	18	10	9	4	4
Australia	1961–64	207	1,581	1	113	528	14
	1985–86	145	206	19	116	322	15
Canada	1961–64	228	526	49	78	423	16
	1985–86	244	682	95	92	299	13
Mexico	1961–64	183	13	2	25	64	4
	1985–86	163	69	48	36	104	11
New Zealand	1961–64	134	96	1	115	1,236	18
	1985–86	158	171	17	133	1,245	16
United States	1961–64	146	512	130	92	298	20
	1985–86	234	571	240	110	277	17

Note: a The estimates of indirect grain consumption via livestock assume that no rice is used in feedmixes.
Source: International Economic Data Bank, *Agricultural Trade Tapes*, ANU, Canberra, 1990.

other than wheat, soybean and dairy products has remained high (Table 7). This is partly because per capita consumption of livestock products is still very low in ASEAN relative to other countries (Table 8). Should those consumption levels rise as ASEAN incomes grow, there is very considerable scope for growth in their imports of either livestock feedstuffs and/or livestock end products as the comparative advantage of the large agricultural suppliers (Indonesia and Thailand) continues to move rapidly towards light manufactures such as textiles and clothing (Tables 3 and 5).

China's agricultural production growth has slowed considerably in recent years, following the initial boost to yields that resulted from the increase in producer prices, the freeing of rural markets and, especially, the introduction of the household responsibility system in rural areas. Given that China's crop yields are already quite high by world standards (see Table 5), farm productivity growth in the 1990s is likely to be slower than in the late 1970s and early 1980s unless producer prices are again increased substantially. Indeed, if urban reforms were to improve incentives in non-farm activities and to allow rural-to-urban migration, there may well be a 'de-agriculturalisation' in China of the sort predicted by booming sector theory and experienced in Korea and Taiwan in the 1960s and 1970s.

The equations in the second section of this paper predict quite accurately agriculture's shares of employment and GDP for China in 1986. They might therefore be used to project those shares for the year 2000. A conservative scenario could be GDP and population growing at 6 and 1.7 per cent, respectively, while an optimistic scenario could involve growth rates of 9 per cent for GDP and 1.3 per cent for population. In the conservative scenario the employment share would fall from 61 to 50 per cent between 1986 and the year 2000, while in the optimistic growth scenario it would fall to 43 per cent, according to those equations. The GDP share would likewise fall, from 31 per cent in 1986 to 25 per cent in the conservative case and to 20 per cent in the optimistic case. Tyers and Anderson (1991, ch.7) use their model of world food markets to see what these growth rates would mean for China's production and trade of particular commodities. Assuming that real prices of farm products are held constant through the 1990s in China, the agricultural policies of other countries are not altered, and the income elasticities of demand and price-independent productivity growth rates are as shown at the top of Table 9, China's food consumption, self-sufficiency and trade levels are projected to be as shown in the lower parts of that table.

Even though the model used provides no more than a consistent framework for projecting trends given specific assumptions, it nonetheless provides results which can illustrate several points. First, in the conservative scenario China's self-sufficiency in these foods would continue to decline, even for livestock products, despite the large increase in import dependence on feedgrains (and soybean, not shown in these results). Second, in the optimistic scenario, in which both agricultural and non-agricultural production are assumed to grow 50 per cent faster, food self-sufficiency nonetheless still drops to 90 per cent because the faster production growth happens to be roughly matched by faster consumption growth (particularly of feedgrains by the livestock industries), given the higher rate of growth of real incomes in that scenario. And third, while China's grain imports would become much larger in the optimistic scenario (up to one-third instead of one-fifth of world trade in coarse grain

Table 9 Food consumption, self-sufficiency and trade of China, 1965 to 2000

	Wheat	Coaqrse grain	Rice	Ruminant meat	Non-ruminant meat	Dairy products	Sugar	Weighted average
Parameter assumptions								
Income elasticity of direct demand	0.5	0.1	0.1	1.1	1	1.2	1	
Price-independent productivity growth rate (% p.a.)								
— Conservative	3.5	2.5	2	5	5	5	5	
— Optimistic	5.2	3.7	2	7.5	7.5	7.5	7.5	
Per capita consumption (kg p.a.)								
Actual 1965–69	41	64	84	0.4	8	3	3	
Actual 1985–86	97	84	117	1	18	5	7	
Projected 2000								
— Conservative	132	130	119	2.1	31	9	11	
— Optimistic	159	184	123	3.1	41	13	16	
Self-sufficiency (%)								
Actual 1970–74	93	104	105	98	101	100	79	102
Actual 1985–86	87	96	100	99	104	98	80	96
Projected 2000								
— Conservative	75	73	101	82	97	92	91	90
— Optimistic	78	62	102	78	89	87	87	90
Imports net of exports (mmt)								
Actual 1970–74	5	1	-2	0	-0.2	0	0.6	
Actual 1985–86	8	-4	-1	0	-0.2	0.1	1.5	
Projected 2000								
— Conservative	45	48	-1	0.1	2.6	1	1.3	
— Optimistic	46	94	-2	0.4	2	2.3	2.9	
% difference between conservative and optimistic scenarios in the year 2000 in:								
International price	4	5	1	2	-1	2	6	
World trade volume	-1	14	1	1	2	0	3	

Source: Tyers & Anderson (1991, Tables 8.5, 8.6, 8.7 & 8.9).

in 2000, for example), the effect of this greater import volume on the international price of grain is relatively minor—no more than 5 per cent (see bottom of Table 9). This is attributable to the flexibility of the world's agricultural producers in substituting out of one product and into another as market conditions change.

The continuing growth in import demand for agricultural products by East Asia, and in their export supply of manufactured goods, ensures that the land-abundant countries of North

America and Australasia will continue to enjoy a comparative advantage in producing food, feed and fibre for those (and other) markets. However, the composition of that import growth will depend importantly on the extent to which livestock production is protected from import competition in East Asia.

Prospective policy changes

The above discussion is premised on a continuation of current policy trends (apart from the discussion of a possible return by China to its reform agenda). There are, however, several prospective policy changes in the next decade or so which could affect those projected patterns of production and trade. Five such developments that come to mind are: the Uruguay Round and associated GATT activities; the tendency towards more nationalism and regionalism; developments within Europe in particular; possible reforms in Indo-China and North Korea; and the greening of world politics.[12]

(i) The Uruguay Round and associated GATT activities. A critical aspect of the Uruguay Round involves the negotiation of reductions in agricultural and other protectionism, particularly in OECD countries. The direct stakes are quite high: according to one recent study, a 50 per cent phased reduction in OECD agricultural protection during the 1990s would yield a net benefit to OECD countries of US$36 billion per year (in 1985 dollars) by the year 2000 (Anderson and Tyers 1990b). However, the indirect stakes are far higher, because the US negotiators in particular insist that the prospects for liberalising non-farm trade in this round depend heavily on a liberalising outcome for agriculture. If the round does conclude at the end of 1990 with a significant liberalisation of both farm and non-farm trade, and if in addition the Multifibre Arrangement (which expires in mid-1991) is replaced with a more liberal agreement on textile and clothing trade that is brought into the mainstream of the GATT, one can expect to see more specialisation in production and trade and faster economic growth rates globally. This would accelerate East Asia's industrial development, *ceteris paribus*, and increase that region's capacity to import more food, feed and fibre from producers in North America, Australasia and elsewhere. It is to be hoped that the locking in of negotiations on non-farm trade liberalisation with those for agriculture in the Uruguay Round will be sufficient incentive for the governments of agricultural protectionist countries to lower their farm support despite the strong domestic political opposition from farmers discussed in the third section above.

(ii) Nationalist and regionalist tendencies. The slow economic growth of the 1980s has encouraged an increase in nationalism, notably in the United States. There has also been an increased emphasis on regionalism, largely in response to the increasing economic integration associated with the Europe 1992 program in Western Europe. It has manifest itself in the Australia–New Zealand free-trade agreement as well as in the US bilateral trade agreements with Canada, Israel, the Caribbean and, prospectively, Mexico and other Latin American countries. It is also manifesting itself in regional negotiations, most notably among North American and Western Pacific countries (the latest acronym for which is APEC — Asia–Pacific Economic Cooperation).

While such bilateral and regional arrangements run the risk of diverting rather than expanding trade (Krugman 1989), some of them at least are likely to expand trade. Indeed, the APEC initiative is specifically aimed at encouraging trade and investment on a non-discriminatory most-favoured-nation basis and supporting multilateralism through the GATT system (Drysdale and Garnaut 1989).

Moreover, the nationalist and regionalist tendencies are being offset — and perhaps will be more than offset in the 1990s — by a strong tendency towards internationalism. This is resulting from two sources. One is the growth of intra-firm international trade of multinational corporations. For example, even apparel firms in the United States are becoming ambivalent about US import barriers, which may inhibit the growth of their offshore export-oriented operations. The other is the blossoming of specialised service industries, such as international banking and insurance, whose growth is tied to the expansion in international trade. Both of these groups of producers are becoming ever-stronger advocates for the strengthening of GATT rules and disciplines. This tendency increases the prospects for liberalising world trade and hence for greater specialisation in production and exports, including in farm products. Traditional agricultural-exporting countries would obviously gain if the relative price of farm products rose as a consequence of such liberalisation. But, in addition, recent research suggests that so too would many developing countries that are net food importers, particularly if agricultural innovation is price-responsive (Anderson and Tyers 1990a).

(iii) Developments within Europe. What are the likely implications for Pacific Rim agriculture of developments in Europe? The Europe 1992 program of eliminating barriers between the twelve member states of the European Community, the unification of the two Germanys, the granting of EC associate member status to nearby non-EC countries, and the dramatic reforms in Eastern Europe are developments that are becoming increasingly

intertwined.[13] A probable effect of the Europe 1992 program will be increased specialization of production within the European Community and faster economic growth there. It remains to be seen whether all internal barriers to agricultural trade (for example, those due to the use of Monetary Compensatory Amounts) will be eliminated and whether national governments will resist the temptation to replace them with national farm support programs to maintain current protection levels. In the event that internal barriers are removed and governments limit themselves to adjustment assistance to farmers, then production would expand in the lowest-cost areas of the European Community at the expense of high-cost areas. Whether this in combination with the rest of the Europe 1992 program would expand or contract the net agricultural export surplus of the European Community — and hence its impact on Pacific and other economies — is an empirical question requiring detailed multi-country computable general equilibrium modelling of the European Community.

The unification of the two Germanys raises many complex issues and questions. Given that East Germany has twice as much agricultural land per capita as its neighbour, its grain yields per hectare are only five-sixths of those in West Germany, and it is poorer and so has a much larger share of its workforce in agriculture, an increase in the relative price of farm products in the east to the levels operating in the west may well stimulate a considerable expansion in farm output. This would have the initial effect of expanding Europe's excess supply of food and so driving down international food prices. Over the longer term, however, East Germany's income growth would lead to an expansion in domestic food consumption, and the inflow of industrial capital would strengthen its comparative advantage in manufacturing relative to agriculture in the way described in the first section of this paper.

Reforms in the rest of Eastern Europe might be expected to be similar though much less rapid than those in East Germany. The sequencing of market reform will of course have an important bearing on the medium-term outcome: if agricultural markets are reformed first, as was done in China, then net export surpluses of farm products might expand initially. But since these economies have barely half as much agricultural land per worker as the rest of the world and their real per capita incomes and wages are perhaps no more than a quarter of those in Western Europe, their comparative advantage would soon switch to relatively labour-intensive standard manufactures. Therefore, provided their domestic agricultural prices do not rise above international levels and their non-agricultural markets are also liberalised, they are likely to be competing with East Asian suppliers for markets for manufactured goods in Western Europe and North America. And this would be even more likely should they get preferential access to EC markets (as may associate members of the European Community such as Turkey). This may dampen prospects for export expansion from East Asia's NIEs, particularly if the EC member states of Southern Europe demand increased external barriers to non-European imports of labour-intensive manufactures as a *quid pro quo* for tolerating preferential access of East European goods to EC markets (Hamilton 1991). Any such dampening would in turn slow East Asia's growth in import demand for farm products and so reduce the export prospects of farmers in North America and Australasia. Moreover, a proliferation of preferential trading arrangements in Europe may also weaken the GATT system of world trade in general. This too would be detrimental to the interests of Pacific Rim countries.

(iv) Reforms in Indo-China and North Korea. If China's growth experience of the 1980s and the ending of the Cold War between the superpowers had the effect of stimulating economic reforms in and the opening up of Indo-China and North Korea, how would agricultural trade be affected? Indo-China undoubtedly would be initially a net agricultural exporter. Indeed, an increase in rice exports from Vietnam has become apparent recently. If Vietnam was opened up further and grew rapidly it may not be too many years before this country of 63 million people began to transform its comparative advantage towards unskilled labour-intensive manufactures, however, given that it has barely one-quarter as much agricultural land per capita as neighbouring Thailand (see Table 1).

North Korea has, like South Korea, a productive workforce and relatively little agricultural land. If opened up it would be likely to follow a pattern of trade and development similar to South Korea but a few years behind it. That is, it would become increasingly dependent on agricultural imports as it exploited its comparative advantage in (initially light) manufactures. Its market would be no more than half the size of South Korea's, however, given the population difference.

(v) The greening of world politics. The dramatic increase in recent years in the concern for the environment, both locally and globally, will impact on Pacific and world production and trade in a number of important ways. One immediate effect is the increase in concern for chemical residues in what we eat. In Western Europe this is manifesting itself in calls for the banning of imports of US beef that has been produced with growth hormones. The fear is that this legitimate concern of consumers will be used to excess by agricultural protectionist interests, leading to a proliferation of such trade restrictions. As more information becomes available on the extent of the harmful effects of such chemicals, and on their presence in

domestic as well as foreign food, one might expect to see consumers demand and be prepared to pay more for low-chemical foods. This would strengthen the agricultural comparative advantage of countries which use few chemicals (Australia, New Zealand and Thailand) at the expense of countries whose farming is relatively chemical-intensive (Japan and Western Europe). With incomplete information there may also be a bias by consumers with respect to imported food in favour of produce from advanced as distinct from developing countries.

A second direct consequence of greater environmental awareness is the likelihood, especially in densely populated countries, that people will oppose the use of chemicals in farming and the intensive production of livestock because of the pollution it causes to local air and water. As it becomes more generally recognised that high product prices stimulate these polluting activities, sympathy of non-farmers towards agricultural protection in Western Europe and Japan will weaken. This too will enhance the farm export prospects of both lightly populated countries, such as Australia and New Zealand, and developing countries more prepared to tolerate such pollution.

In addition, there are some other consequences of the greening of world politics that may indirectly affect agricultural development and trade. In countries which introduce taxes on industrial pollution, the production of non-industrial goods, including farm products, may well expand. Pollution-intensive industries will thus tend to be relocated to developing countries, assuming the pollution-abatement costs imposed are positively correlated with the countries' per capita incomes. *Ceteris paribus*, this effect will reduce the tendency for agricultural comparative advantage to move from advanced to developing countries in the course of global economic growth.

Trade will also be affected by the increasing awareness that pollution extends beyond national boundaries and has significant regional and global consequences. The relocation of heavy industrial activity from West to East Europe and from Japan and Korea to the north coast of China certainly has not eliminated the polluting effects of those industries from the viewpoint of the more advanced economies, because pollution is carried back by the rivers and prevailing winds. And the emission of greenhouse gases and the damage to the ozone layer have truly global consequences, such as rising temperatures and sea levels and altered rainfall patterns. Clearly, the latter will affect agricultural production and trade directly.[14] But it may also affect farm trade indirectly insofar as it leads to attempts to set new international rules relating to environmental damage. There will be strong free-rider incentives for firms not to abide by such rules, so economic sanctions will be required to enforce compliance by offending nations. Given the emotionally charged nature of debates on the environment, it would not be surprising if first-best policy instruments were not used for coping with this problem. Most likely, the sanctions would take the form of restrictions on trade and investment flows, which could seriously weaken the world trading system under the GATT and have adverse consequences for global resource allocation and economic growth. People involved in the setting and policing of rules aimed at maintaining a liberal world trade regime may need to be thinking sooner rather than later about how to respond to this likely change in international relations (Whalley 1990).

Conclusion

The standard theory of trade and development outlined in the first section of this paper is certainly helpful in understanding what has happened, and what is likely to happen, to agriculture in Pacific Rim economies, given details or assumptions about the openness and the growth rates of those economies. What that theory does not provide, however, is an understanding of what determines whether and when an insular country will choose to open its economy (as did Japan in 1868, South Korea and Taiwan in the early 1960s, China in 1978, and parts of Eastern Europe from the late 1980s). Nor does it explain the differing growth rates across countries, other than to point to the strong statistical correlation between openness and economic growth as evidence to support the gains from trade argument.

A better understanding of the dynamics of economic development is still clearly needed. Thankfully, a resurgence of research on the topic has begun, in three distinct but closely related areas. The 'new' trade theories emphasising economies of scale and imperfect competition have shown theoretically and empirically that the gains from trade liberalisation may be very much larger than our constant returns to scale and perfect competition models suggest. That is, they provide results that are closer to what trade economists instinctively believe to be the very substantial benefits of openness.[15]

Second, the 'new' growth theories are seeking to understand the mechanisms by which economic growth and development are generated. They are addressing such questions as: why do we not observe more capital flowing from capital-abundant to capital-poor countries, and what determines the rates of product innovation and international technology transfer?[16]

And third, the 'new' economics of politics is improving our understanding of why governments adopt the policies they do, and hence of what is required to change policies, and the rules that govern policy-making, to encourage economic growth.[17]

A particularly important political economy question to address with the help of this literature is: under what conditions will protection to declining industries such as agriculture cease growing or reverse? There have been a few dramatic instances of the complete withdrawal of government support to industry, such as for Swedish steel production and shipbuilding in the 1970s and for its textile and clothing industries from 1992, as well as for the US footwear industry. Cassing and Hillman (1986) suggest that aggregate political support from a protected declining industry may dwindle as the industry contracts until a point is reached where that support is less than the political opposition to that protection from other groups who are hurt by it. At that point protection could be fully withdrawn.

Another reason protection may be reduced is because of a shock to the political markets for protection policies. A recent example is the trade friction arising from Northeast Asia's current account surpluses and the US twin deficits, which led to US pressure on Northeast Asia's domestic markets to reduce protection on beef and other agricultural products. The liberalisation of trade in those products, which is scheduled to occur in the 1990s, would almost certainly not have occurred without the addition of US pressure (Lee, Hadwinger & Lee 1990). A second example is the growing realisation that pollution from the use of agricultural chemicals is correlated with agricultural price levels, leading to environmentalists adding a new voice of opposition to agricultural protection for that reason too.

Third and finally, there is the prospect of protection reductions though the setting of new rules, for example under the GATT. The extent and cost of agricultural protection escalated in the 1980s, galvanising GATT contracting parties to place agriculture high on the agenda of the Uruguay Round of trade policy negotiations. Part of the motivation came from a realisation of two facts. One was that the presence of new GATT rules limiting agricultural protection would make it easier for governments to deny farm lobbies further support — and even to wind back existing support. The other fact was that if all countries liberalised simultaneously, international food prices would rise and so the extent of price decline needed to reduce protection to a particular level would be less. Indeed, even if protection levels were as much as halved over the 1990s, agricultural production levels would still expand somewhat in virtually all OECD countries, according to recent simulation results (Anderson and Tyers 1990b).

If the Uruguay Round is successful in having countries agree to limit their agricultural support programs, improved monitoring and dispute settlement mechanisms will need to be established. Such mechanisms would have the additional advantage of increasing the transparency of policies, thereby making it less costly for domestic groups harmed by distortionary policies to oppose them in future (Spriggs 1990). Whether countries are prepared to give up their sovereignty over agricultural policies to that extent, however, is something that only time will tell.

Notes

* Helpful comments from Bill Coyle, John Dyck and other IATRC (International Agricultural Trade Research Consortium) symposium participants on the first draft of this paper are gratefully acknowledged. Since completing this paper the author has joined the economic research staff of the GATT Secretariat in Geneva. The views expressed are the author's own and are not intended to reflect the view of the GATT Secretariat or GATT contracting parties.

1 The weight of empirical evidence supports the view that agricultural prices have declined relative to industrial product prices during the past century or so, although the difficulty of accounting for changing qualities of manufactured goods needs to be kept in mind (Spraos 1980; Sapsford 1985; Grilli and Yang 1988). This suggests that the outward shift in the supply curve for non-food products compared to food products has not been fast enough to offset the relatively slow growth in demand for the latter.

2 Available evidence suggests that the income elasticity of demand for services (which make up the vast majority of non-tradables) is well above unity in developing countries and tends towards unity as incomes grow (Lluch, Powell and Williams 1977; Kravis, Heston and Summers 1983; Theil and Clements 1987). So if productivity growth is no more rapid for non-tradables than for tradables — indeed it is probably slower (see Clark 1957) — but demand for non-tradables expands more rapidly while demand for tradables expands less rapidly than aggregate output, both the price and the quantity of non-tradables relative to tradables will increase. Strong across-country evidence that the price of non-tradables relative to tradables increases with real incomes is provided in Kravis and Lipsey (1988).

3 The agricultural growth bias in this economy has to be strong enough not only to offset the decline in the international price of food relative to prices of other tradables but also to offset the pull of resources into the production of non-tradables (Anderson 1987).

4 See also Deardorff (1984), Eaton (1987), Leamer (1987) and Balassa and Bauwens (1988).

5 For discussion of why so little capital flows from capital-abundant to capital-scarce economies even when there are no government-imposed barriers to such flows, see Lucas (1990). The present analysis also begs the question of what determines rates of savings, investment and technology trade, issues which are currently being grappled with by the 'new' growth theorists. See, for example, Grossman and Helpman (1990a, 1990b) and the references cited therein.

6 Since many empirical studies are available with such evidence, only a small sample of evidence is presented here. For more detailed evidence, see Kuznets (1971) and Chenery, Robinson and Syrquin (1986), for example.

7 For space reasons smaller economies are not discussed here, but the largest of those omitted — Papua New Guinea — is analysed in Jarrett and Anderson (1989). Until very

recently Central and South American countries have not been closely involved in Pacific Rim discussions and so are also omitted here, although they are examined in Anderson (1983).

8 Canned, dried and frozen fruit and vegetables and powdered and UHT vacuum-packed fluid milk are of course close substitutes for the fresh produce and can be traded internationally. The c.i.f. price of imports of such substitutes would thus determine the ceiling on domestic prices of the fresh products in the absence of import restrictions.

9 Anderson and Tyers (1986) estimate the following regression equation for 30 countries/country groups spanning the world (t-values in parentheses):

$$\underset{}{NPC} = \underset{(8.7)}{0.22} + \underset{(5.6)}{0.11\,YPC} - \underset{(-10.7)}{0.51\,CA} \qquad \bar{R}^2 = 0.83$$

where NPC is the log of the weighted average nominal agricultural protection coefficient in 1980–82; YPC is the log of the ratio of an economy's per capita income to the global average per capita income in 1982; and CA is the log of the food self-sufficiency ratio at global free-trade prices as estimated by the authors' model of world food markets. The main exceptions to the rule that rich countries subsidise agriculture are the agricultural-exporting countries of Australia and New Zealand, while important exceptions to the opposite rule for developing countries are the food-importing economies of Korea and Taiwan. All four economies have extreme values for CA and so are not inconsistent with the above political economy theory.

10 In what follows it is assumed that the current macroeconomic problems of East Asia's surpluses and the US twin deficits are solved through appropriate adjustments to monetary, fiscal and exchange rate policies.

11 The combined effects of East Asia's fuel-conservation measures, its adjustment away from energy-intensive activities, and the decline in international energy prices in the 1980s can be seen from data on the share of petroleum in the value of East Asia's imports. In 1980–82 that share was 36 per cent in Japan, 25 per cent in Korea and 21 per cent in Taiwan, but by 1988 those shares were only 10, 7 and 5 per cent, respectively. The earlier adjustments to high prices puts these economies in a much sounder position to cope with subsequent petroleum price hikes such as in late 1990.

12 Also of importance is the 1990 US farm bill, but I leave that to more qualified analysts. The recently announced liberalisation of Japanese and Korean imports of beef and other farm products are important too, but their likely effects are fairly obvious.

13 In the interests of brevity, the great uncertainty associated with developments in the Soviet Union is not discussed here.

14 One preliminary attempt to quantify these effects is reported in the study by Kane, Reilly and Bucklin (1989).

15 See, for example, Helpman & Krugman (1985) and the survey by Richardson (1989).

16 See, for example, Grossman & Helpman (1990a, 1990b), Lucas (1978, 1980) and Romer (1990).

17 See, for example, Baldwin (1989), Magee, Brock & Young (1989), Hillman (1989) and Jones & Krueger (1989) on endogenous trade policies; Brennan & Buchanan (1985) on the designing of rules for government; and Olson (1982) on politico-economic reasons for the slowing of growth in OECD countries.

References

ABARE (1990) *Agriculture and Resources Quarterly* Vol. 2, No. 1 (March) Canberra: Australian Bureau of Agricultural and Resource Economics

Anderson, K. (1983) 'Economic growth, comparative advantage and agricultural trade of Pacific Rim countries' *Review of Marketing and Agricultural Economics* Vol. 51, No. 3: 231–48 (December); also published in G.E. Schuh & J.L. McCoy (eds) *Food, Agriculture and Development in the Pacific Basin* (ch. 2) Boulder: Westview Press

——— (1987) 'On why agriculture declines with economic growth' *Agricultural Economics* Vol. 1, No. 3: 195–207 (June)

——— (1989) 'Rent-seeking and price-distorting policies in rich and poor countries', Seminar Paper No. 428, Institute for International Economic Studies, University of Stockholm (January)

——— (1990) *Changing Comparative Advantages in China: Effects on Food, Feed and Fibre Markets* Paris: OECD

——— (ed) (1991) *New Silk Roads: East Asia and World Textiles Markets* Cambridge: Cambridge University Press (forthcoming)

Anderson, K., Y. Hayami & others (1986) *The Political Economy of Agricultural Protection: East Asia in International Perspective* Boston, London & Sydney: Allen & Unwin

Anderson, K. & R. Tyers (1986) 'Agricultural policies of industrial countries and their effects on traditional food exporters' *Economic Record* Vol. 62, No. 179: 385–99 (December)

——— (1990a) 'Welfare gains to developing countries from food trade liberalization following the Uruguay Round', mimeo, University of Adelaide (July)

——— (1990b) 'Effects of tariffication of food trade barriers following the Uruguay Round' Seminar Paper 90–02, Centre for International Economic Studies, University of Adelaide (May)

Balassa, B. (1965) 'Trade liberalization and "revealed" comparative advantage' *Manchester School of Economic and Social Studies* Vol. 33, No. 2: 99–124 (May)

——— (1979) 'The changing pattern of comparative advantage in manufactured goods' *Review of Economics and Statistics* Vol. 61, No. 2: 259–66 (May)

Balassa, B. & L. Bauwens (1988) *Changing Trade Patterns in Manufactured Goods: An Econometric Investigation* Amsterdam: North–Holland

Baldwin, R.E. (1989) 'The political economy of trade policy' *Journal of Economic Perspectives* Vol. 3, No. 4: 119–35 (Fall)

Bowen, H.P. (1983) 'Changes in the international distribution of resources and their impact on US comparative advantage' *Review of Economics and Statistics* Vol. 65, No. 3: 402–14 (August)

Brennan, G. & J.M. Buchanan (1985) *The Reason of Rules* Cambridge: Cambridge University Press

Cassing, J.H. & A.L. Hillman (1986) 'Shifting comparative advantage and senescent industry collapse' *American Economic Review* Vol. 76, No. 3: 516–23 (June)

Chenery, H., S. Robinson & M. Syrquin (1986) *Industrialization and Growth: A Comparative Study* New York: Oxford University Press (for the World Bank)

Clark, C. (1957) *The Conditions of Economic Progress* London: Macmillan (3rd edition)

Corden, W.M. (1984) 'Booming sector and Dutch disease economics: survey and consolidation' *Oxford Economic Papers* No. 36: 359–80

Deardorff, A.V. (1984) 'An exposition and exploration of Krueger's trade model' *Canadian Journal of Economics* Vol. 17, No. 4: 731–46 (November)

Drysdale, P. & R. Garnaut (1989) 'A Pacific free trade area?' in J. Schott (ed) *Free Trade Areas and US Trade Policy* Washington DC: Institute for International Economics

Eaton, J. (1987) 'A dynamic specific-factors model of international trade' *Review of Economic Studies* Vol. 54, No. 2: 325–38 (April)

Freebairn, J. (1987) 'The natural resource industries' in R. Maddock & I. McLean (eds) *The Australian Economy in the Long Run* (ch. 6) Cambridge: Cambridge University Press

Garnaut, R. (1989) *Australia and the Northeast Asian Ascendancy* Canberra: Australian Government Publishing Service

Grilli, E.R. & M.C. Yang (1988) 'Primary commodity prices, manufactured goods prices, and the terms of trade of developing countries: what the long run shows' *World Bank Economic Review* Vol. 2, No. 1: 1–48 (January)

Grossman, G.M. & E. Helpman (1990a) 'Trade, innovation and growth' *American Economic Review* Vol. 80, No. 2: 86–91 (May)

——— (1990b) 'Comparative advantage and long-run growth' *American Economic Review* Vol. 80 (forthcoming)

Hamilton, C. (1990) 'The new Silk Road to Europe: new directions for old trade' Seminar Paper 89–07, Centre for International Economic Studies, University of Adelaide (November); forthcoming in K. Anderson (ed) *New Silk Roads: East Asia and world textile markets* (ch. 8) Cambridge: Cambridge University Press

Helpman, E. & P.R. Krugman (1985) *Market Structure and Foreign Trade* Cambridge: MIT Press

Hillman, A.L. (1989) *The Political Economy of Protection* New York: Harwood Academic Publishers

Jarrett, F.G. & K. Anderson (1989) *Growth, Structural Change and Economic Policy in Papua New Guinea: Implications for Agriculture* Canberra: National Centre for Development Studies, Australian National University

Johnson, H.G. (1968) *Comparative Cast and Commercial Policy Theory for a Developing World Economy* Stockholm: Almqvist & Wiksell

Johnson, D.G. (1973) *World Agriculture in Disarray* London: Fontana

Jones, R. & A. Krueger (eds) (1989) *The Political Economy of International Trade* Oxford: Basil Blackwell

Kane, S., J. Reilly & R. Bucklin (1989) 'Implications of the greenhouse effect for world agricultural commodity markets' USDA paper presented at the Western Economic Association Conference, Lake Tahoe (June)

Keating, M. (1973) *The Australian Workforce 1910–11 to 1960–61* Canberra: ANU Press

Keesing, D.B. & D.R. Sherk (1971) 'Population density in patterns of trade and development' *American Economic Review* Vol. 61, No. 5: 956–61 (December)

Klein, L.R. (1990) 'The economics of turning swords into plowshares' *Challenge* 18–26 (March–April)

Kravis, I.B., W. Heston & R. Summers (1983) 'The share of services in economic growth' in F.G. Adams & B.G. Hickman (eds) *Global Econometrics* Cambridge: MIT Press

Kravis, I.B. & R.E. Lipsey (1988) 'National price levels and the prices of tradeables and nontradables' *American Economic Review* Vol. 78, No. 2: 474–8 (May)

Krueger, A. (1977) *Growth, Distortions and Patterns of Trade Among Many Countries* Princeton, NJ: International Finance Section

——— (1990) 'Asian trade and growth lessons' *American Economic Review* Vol. 80, No. 2: 108–12 (May)

Krugman, P. (1989) 'Is bilateralism bad?' *NBER Working Paper* No. 2972, Cambridge, Mass. (May)

Kuznets, S.S. (1971) *Economic Growth of Nations: Total Output and Production Structure* Cambridge: Harvard University Press

Leamer, E.E. (1984) *Sources of International Comparative Advantage: Theory and Evidence* Cambridge: MIT Press

——— (1987) 'Paths of development in the three-factor, n-good general equilibrium model' *Journal of Political Economy* Vol. 95, No. 5: 961–99 (October)

Lee, Y.S., D.F. Hadwinger & C.B. Lee (1990) 'Agricultural policy making under international pressures' *Food Policy* Vol. 15, No. 5: 418–33 (October)

Lluch, C., A.A. Powell & R.A. Williams (1977) *Patterns in Household Demand and Savings* New York: Oxford University Press

Lucas, R.E. (1988) 'On the mechanics of economic development' *Journal of Monetary Economics* Vol. 22, No. 1: 3–42

——— (1990) 'Why doesn't capital flow from rich to poor countries?' *American Economic Review* Vol. 80, No. 2: 92–6 (May)

Magee, S.P., W.A. Brock & L. Young (1989) *Black Hole Tariffs and Endogenous Policy Theory: Political Economy in General Equilibrium* Cambridge: Cambridge University Press

OECD (1989) *Historical Statistics 1960 – 1987* Paris: OECD

Olson, M. (1982) *The Rise and Decline of Nations: Economic Growth, Stagflation and Social Rigidities* New Haven: Yale University Press

Perkins, D.H. (1988) 'Reforming China's economic system' *Journal of Economic Literature* Vol. 26, No. 2: 601–45 (June)

Richardson, H.D. (1989) 'Empirical research on trade liberalization with imperfect competition' *OECD Economic Studies* No. 12: 7–51 (Spring)

Romer, P.M. (1990) 'Endogenous technological change' *Journal of Political Economy* Vol. 98, No. 5: 571–102

Sapsford, D. (1985) 'The statistical debate on the net barter terms of trade between primary commodities and manufactures: a comment and some additional evidence' *Economic Journal* Vol. 95, No. 379: 781–8 (September)

Schultz, T.W. (ed) (1978) *Distortions of Agricultural Incentives* Bloomington: Indiana University Press

Spraos, J. (1980) 'The statistical debate on the net barter terms of trade between primary commodities and manufactures' *Economic Journal* Vol. 90, No. 357: 107–28 (March)

Spriggs, J.D. (1990) 'Transparency vs protectionism' Seminar Paper 90–03, Centre for International Economic Studies, University of Adelaide (June)

Theil, H. & K.W. Clements (1987) *Applied Demand Analysis: Results From System-Wide Approaches* Cambridge, Mass: Ballinger

Tyers, R. & K. Anderson (1991) *Disarray in World Food Markets* Cambridge: Cambridge University Press (forthcoming)

US Department of Commerce (1976) *Historical Statistics of the United States* (bicentennial edition) Washington DC: US Department of Commerce

Whalley, J. (1990) 'Environmental protection and international trade' Paper presented to a conference on The Economics of Environmental Policy, Canberra, 11–12 October

World Bank (1988a) *World Development Report 1988* New York: Oxford University Press

——— (1988b) *The World Bank Atlas 1988* Washington DC: The World Bank

——— (1990) *World Development Report 1990* New York: Oxford University Press

Recently published Pacific Economic Papers:

197 Open regionalism: a key to East Asia's economic future
Peter Drysdale, July 1991

196 Japanese corporate tax policy and direct investment abroad
Yasushi Iwamoto, June 1991

195 A market share analysis of Japanese beef imports
Julian B. Morison, May 1991

194 Dangō: Japan's price-fixing conspiracies
John McMillan, April 1991

193 Financial reform in China and Hong Kong 1978–89: a comparative overview
Y. C. Jao, March 1991

192 Implications of China's foreign exchange system for the wool market
Will Martin, February 1991

191 Can Japan and the Soviet Union sort out their differences?
J.A.A. Stockwin, January 1991

190 Japan as a creditor: macroeconomic issues
H.W. Arndt, December 1990

189 Macroeconomic management in the Pacific: growth and external stability
Ross Garnaut, November 1990

Annual subscription rate for twelve issues:

Individuals $A40.00
Institutions $A100.00

Cost for single issues:

$A15.00
$A10.00 (Students)

All prices include postage (surface mail)

Available from: Publications Department
Australia–Japan Research Centre
Research School of Pacific Studies
The Australian National University
GPO Box 4, Canberra ACT 2601, Australia
Facsimile: 06–249-0767
Telephone: 06–249-3780